TO LIGHTEN MY HOUSE

To Lighten My House

ALASTAIR REID

poems

MORGAN & MORGAN Publishers
SCARSDALE   NEW YORK

ACKNOWLEDGEMENTS

The following poems: Poem Without Ends—Maine Coast—
Isle of Arran—The Waterglass, under the title of The Glass Town—
and The Village—were first published in the New Yorker.
A number of other poems in the book have previously appeared in
the Atlantic Monthly, Wake, The Scots Review, and Blast.
The drawings are reproduced with permission of the
Curt Valentin Gallery, New York.
      To all of these, acknowledgements are due.

Drawings—KURT ROESCH

POEMS

I

POEM WITHOUT ENDS

One cannot take the beginning out of the air
saying 'It is the time: the hour is here'.
The process is continuous as wind,
the bird observed, not rising, but in flight,
unrealized, in motion in the mind.

The end of everything is similar, never
actually happening, but always over.
The agony, the bent head, only tell
that already in the heart the innocent evening
is thick with all the ferment of farewell.

POEM FOR MY FATHER

When my father first made me in a Scottish summer
he heard various voices. There was trouble in the islands;
but the act of love was an evening matter, a heart-beat
that ran wild in the blood and swelled and burst and was silence.

So born, I was blessed. The impatient heart-beat hurrying
hard over heather-grown hills, the green wanton sea
splintering wild in the cave and becoming the quiet
wash of the ultimate wave, translating itself into me.

And I think of the quiet way my father had
with his hands which were for blessing, which blessed a tree
unconciously with their touch. And how it was spring on the island
when he reached out and first felt birth: leaves and life: the same mystery.

But then it was different, difficult, with dark weathers engraving
the unlucky island, imposing their winter's worth
of lack: and across the firth the black procession
of blown clouds flying from their unfulfilling north

and sickness running the sullen length of Scotland:
rocks, roots encrusting with years, all the field fallow,
the land unfurrowed, dryness invading our living,
the weight of a war, waste, and worse to follow.

Away now, it becomes a bit of the bone, carving
a cross of a kind, a root in the restless land
when the waves lap over the world and the voices quiver.
Away, the island is a secret held, with hope, in the hand.

But the mind must find its own way back to the bone
and the beginning. Only the blood's blind intellect
tells, when it talks, a truth like stone, corrects
the present, and later leads back to all that this life lacked;

but only begins. Bare rock. And the rest is not only growing,
but building. The inarticulate island offers its choice
of suffering. I choose to achieve the spring, work against winter.
So choosing, I take my vows and become its voice.

And out of the times that tear at the roots, at love,
I begin, with root and with love, to build. And remembering birth,
the act of my father's love, and his faith, I reach
with his hands to bless again the bare potential earth.

LAY FOR NEW LOVERS

In the crux of the dark O under a lemon moon
    lying below the lap of the barn
being lovers we were born   being warm and lovers
and sick with a secret O and the ogling owls
fell sideways out of the thinning dark
and our limbs were liquid and longed to tell
    under the lap of the barn
    in the cup of the dark

In the drip of the day in the early damp of the dawn
    in beads on the brow on the wood of the barn
love over we were worn   being cold and over
and hollow with having loved and the morning birds
were crossing the windows of the early light
and our limbs were lazy and limp with knowing
    under a melon sun
    on the lip of the dawn

In the red of a dawn in the day of an awkward age
    under the cloud of an unconcern
unloving we lie alone   being left and lonely
and lured from a love in the blood now when the hawks
are sweeping a morning out of the simple sky
and we love in a moment left out of the world
    under a slipping sky
    in the sleep of the day

MY ONE HIGH MORNING

My one high morning is the green beginning;
but who could speak across the singing time
of trees and finger-tips where halfwinds worry
a love so easy on the wordless hillside
my anxious sentences all try to climb?

You hold the morning in your hands, its meaning
mostly a song in the blood. I become a tree,
limbs all longing, leaves all eager, loving.
The sap spills out of my root and spells a secret
in sudden green spontaneous certainty.

Currents cross in the lake. Tremendous silence
is all I hold: old words are worn away.
I want to touch and tell your truthful body
this first transforming secret, and awaking
I want to give you all my life away.

BOYHOOD

The day he first began to be boy
was a different shape, was strange. His world was trouble
and trees were shaped like girls as the day grew human and gave him
a handful of painful photographs
to go to bed with in the stinging dark.

The night door closed but never on sleep
while he groped with nightmares in his dogeared pillow
telling his puzzling day under a patchwork cover
to find the easy thread that ravelled
his restless boyhood on a sheet of night.

But every door would burst with morning
wide on a boyish sun and set his feet
chasing a shout across the clear and arrogant fields
under a sky all young and shy with secrets
saved to be solved in the puzzled pillowed dark.

TO LOOK IN THE HEART

It becomes more difficult to look in the heart.
Time brings the easy answer to the tongue.
The eyes learn all the different disguises.
Hands play a simple superficial part.
Even the foot is scarcely once put wrong
and for lover or lawyer, days hold no surprises.

Passion and patience, all are finger-tipped,
held at the end of an eyelash, well-defined.
Only the automatic words are said.
Behind the masks, the skeleton waits, thin-lipped,
while all the clockwork attitudes unwind
and the wasted heart, without a voice, goes dead.

GRANDFATHER

Age was detachment. Out of world and time,
both dead in his bad body, he saved a wind
      with the last of his green love,
ruffled his white-haired years with wizened fingers,
made windy tales from the spells of his sailing life.

Age was release. Past anxious mountains of future
he unbent his graybeard back in an easy strath.
      His words had waterfall strength
when this last blue interval left him a boy's breathing,
and a deep down laughter allowed a joke at death.

Age had no motive. Free of desire and act,
he founded summertimes and doubled dreams
      in between genesis and grief,
and with cleanheaded children close to their first ocean,
lived out in his end the lost boyhood of angels.

THE VILLAGE

This village, like a child's deliberate vision,
shimmers in sunshine. Cottages bloom like flowers
and blink across the gardens thick with silence.
No one moves here but children and ancient women,
and bees haunting the hedges. The village hangs
with more intensity than a heavy dream.

But turn, and you will find the mountains watching
almost in judgment, like stone sentinels
over your shoulder, critical as eyes
behind the screen of distance, keeping watch.
Nor in midsummer ever be deceived
by silence, or by villages at peace.
Behind your house, those hollow hills are hearing
your quietest thoughts, as loud as thunder.

AUTOBIOGRAPHY

A boy, I was content to cling to silence.
The first years found me unprepared for spring.
April spoke quickly with a quick excitement.
My sudden voice was too surprised to sing.

Year followed year, the faithful falling seasons.
My voice was never confident for long.
Now autumn haunts me with the fear of losing
anticipation, and the power of song.

NOT NOW FOR MY SINS' SAKE

Not now for my sins' sake,
nor for Adam or anyone
a memory might wake,
do I take this breaking day to grieve,
not for today's Eve
perpetually weeping in the nibbled apples,
and not for all the lost or too alone.

Not grief for the old-headed children, running
wild in their redletter days,
nor for my longlegged and living girl
dancing to meet me down her fabled ways—
these dear selves shelter in the now of love.

No. Past praise for the world, young once at least,
I come always to grief at last,
not for my death
or the presently splintering world,
but for all failing love
gone waste in words and reasons
down the noiseless tick of the breath,
down all our warring life.
Always again writing my lettered grief,
I hold my changing self, for this instant stilled,
and hold this crisscross world,
love crossed with loss, the cycle of all the sad seasons.

THE DAY THE WEATHER BROKE

Last out in the raining weather, a girl and I
drip in the hazy light while cars slur by,
    and the single drizzling reason
    of rain in an alien season
turns us to each other till a train arrives,
to share, by bond of wetness, our wet lives.

Although, for talk, we can find to put our thumb on
    only the rain in common,
is this what love is — that we draw together
    in the inhuman weather,
Strangers, who pool our sheltered selves and take,
    for the sky's sake,
this luck, to be caught without our usual cloak
    the day the weather broke?

SONG FOR FOUR SEASONS

Held and spelled in a golden fold,
I wished to find a windfall in the orchard —
    held in a summer wind,
I found beyond the well the cidered boys
tempting their sweethearts in the trampled apples.

Going down a dropping autumn sky
I feared to find a spider in the apple —
    going down a falling field,
I found behind the well a longlegged maiden
loving her boy among the stubbled barley.

Stilled and cold in a frozen field,
I hoped to find an apple in the graveyard —
    stilled in a winter waste,
I found beside the drying well a woman
watching the spiders spinning out a shroud.

Climbing a green and growing day,
I grieved to find a grave among the barley —
    climbing a springing hill,
I found above the brimming well a baby
blowing time to pieces on a dandelion.

II

SPELL FOR FIVE FINGERS

The winds and planets beautifully spinning
called for letters and numbers, whirling
    over the counted world.

    I found a world in my hand.
    A five-starred fist of senses
       finger-tipped the time.

    I *found a world in the winds.*
    The elements were seasons
       in the quarters of the heart.

    I found a world in my wishes.
    Head, heart and hand, three guesses.
       My luck went three times round.

    I found a world in the mirror.
    The day and night were doubles.
       My eyes were black and white.

    I *found a world in my head.*
    The sun was one within me.
       My shoulders wore the globe.

One was a word, was a world, was wonder.
Zodiacs, alphabets, calendars tumbled.
The moon made mock of the almanack.
    The maps remembered the weather.
The scale was a spell, the spell was a measure,
the measure was music, the harmony, love —
    and I held the world in a word.
The wonderful numbers spun in a measure.
The letters like lovers were wound in a spell.
The light of the breath was calling the changes
    — and over and over the heart beat time.

THE QUESTION IN THE COBWEB

The frog beneath the juniper
warns us where the terrors are,
crouched below a creaking root
grunts of water underfoot.

Draped on a branch above, the crow
croaks a crude judicial No,
forbidding with a beady eye
any wayward wish to fly.

Furtive flowers in flower beds
hear the wind and bend their heads.
A shiver by the river warns
watch for cows with crooked horns.

A rumble in a tumbled cloud
is mumbling of rain aloud.
A hedgehog humping home alone
makes thunder underneath a stone.

The spider with the knitting legs
purls a puzzle round his eggs.
A nimble stilted centipede
worries a secret in a seed.

Waving leaves like windmill sails,
the tallest elms are telling tales.
A rumour in the garrulous grass
plays havoc with the weatherglass.

Somewhere clocks begin to chime,
telling what we think is time;
meanwhile, the sundial on the lawn
is baffled by the falling sun.

The meadow with the mayflower hair
breathes a last question on the air,
while overhead the homing bees
buzz with private mysteries.

And like some last inquisitor,
the frog beneath the juniper,
crouching in a question mark,
croaks his password to the dark.

MUSIC BOX

Pricked out on pins of time, a tune from nowhere
whirrs on a hairspring hidden in the ears,
and, listening through a microscope, one hears
a spiderweb of sound plucked out of air.

A little twig-legged dancer in a trance
on wooden tiptoe, wearing a whiff of wool,
pirouettes wildly as a ticking spool
unwinds the inches of her watchspring dance.

Watching, a plump and pumpkin-colored clown,
perched on a miniature wirework music stand,
counts careful waltztime with his pinhead hand,
the baton slowing as the box runs down.

Too small for minds. The image suddenly shatters
as somewhere, clumsily, a great clock clatters.

SATURDAY PARK

With a whiff of a Saturday summer, the park
attracts its people in lazy rows.
The pigeons perform and the squirrels eat bark
but most of them gaze at each other's clothes;

and the green goes back and the birds are leaving
and nothing is said, for a stopped hour's sake.
In the midst of the lost there are some of them living —

the little red girl on her roller skate wheels
giving the turning world a try,
and the hobnailed boy showing arrogant heels —
young enough to know why.

DESIGNS FOR THREE DANCERS

I

Her wish explodes in legs,
and through all the hullaballoo hoops of her jumping joy
            come bounding with a growl
the sudden burly goblins of her dream—

      wishes to whirlwinds, a witch to a woman,
      cartwheel capers on a cobwebbed common,
            out of a rafter after a wind,
            streaming a rumour of hair behind
                  to loosen the whims
                  in the windmill limbs
                  as all our alarms
                  come alive as arms,

      and the child in the terrible skin uncovers
      the trace in the trees of the tiptoeing lovers
      who leave in the leaping air, like an angel,
                  the strange little girl
                  on her wing-footed stage
                  (stranger than age)

      while a harp plays havoc and a cello-voiced cow
      remembers and moos to the yellow-eyed daisies
            the ways of an endless loving world
            to the wandered girl in the wishbone curled—

this is the way the muscles sing her name.

II

Once upon America there was a time,
cried the little red hobnailed boy we called Dogear,
        and fell down laughing

and his crazy storybook with its foxed pages
blew into atoms of laughter on a tellpie wind
        and that was the end.

        He was a poet, that boy.

III

No, none of the meadows remember now how her feet
would space them on tiptoe in these mornings of light
down the unprinted grass, princess of air,
fleet-footed, cat-footed, carrying a secret,
light as a falling feather, all alone.
        Through all these days alone
she walked with the weathers turning in her head.

Unwinding a new dance now, in wisps from her feet
she discovers again the spell of her playground days,
the telltale ways of her body, queen of now,
wise as a cat, and wayward to her lover,
old with the fallen world, no more alone.
        So, turning over her life,
she spins through this bright night with a star in her head.

NURSERY SONGS

WHO CAN SAY

Mother, I went to China this morning.
The trees were pagodas, the puddles were seas.
Dragons were hiding behind the begonias.
> I was a mandarin.
> Willows were bowing.
> Lies, lies, said she.
> And I hid from her frightening eyes.
> > *who can say, who can say?*

Children, the gardens belong now to goblins.
The willows spread legends, the waterfall plays.
Fairytales wind like a web round the window.
> Goodnight to all birds now.
> The night's wings are folding.
> Lies, lies, said I.
> But I hid from her wonderful eyes.
> > *who can say, who can say?*

THREE SIDES OF A PENNY

Heads, said the one and the penny spun,
bright as a bullet in the delicate sun.

> *choose choose*
> *win or lose*

Who tells true to the tossing copper?
Nobody guessed at a gust of wind
and the coin came down in the sea.

Tails, said the other and the penny turned over,
hovering in air like a wavering lover.

> *tell tell*
> *head or tail*

Who calls true to the tumbling copper?
No one allowed for a gambling man
and the penny dropped in his hand.

Said the gambling fellow, either will do.
Anyway who split the penny in two?

> *one not two*
> *both are true*

I call yes to the coin in the sky.
One two three and the world goes round —
and he threw the penny away.

NEW HAMPSHIRE

Here, green has grown to be a habit.
The hills are forest-headed, not for farmers.
Trees hug the land as close as fur.
A lake looks naked. There is no way in,

except for local animals. And the roads
stumble and lurch down humps of stubbled dust.
Flowers bloom at ease without being told
and grass has grown untidily, in a hurry.

Here, the tall elm and the leaking maple,
and apple trees as gnarled as farmers' knuckles
ooze stickily with sap or syrup.
Forests are tumbled to make room for trees.

Houses are hewn and hidden in the hedges,
all pine and wooden pegs. The paths are lost.
Towns are a pilgrimage away.
Here, families live alone in hand-made homes.

Only the animals are seasoned owners.
The lakes belong to frogs with broken voices.
Farms are inhabited by rabbits.
A fox barks like a landlord down the dark.

Deer have been known to tiptoe down for apples.
A snake may suddenly scribble out of sight.
Your eyes are never sure. Each evening,
someone comes back from almost seeing a bear.

Here, space is sweet with extra air. The silence
is positive, and has a steady sound.
You seem to own the woods, until
a shotgun coughs, to warn you, in the valley.

A week is a whole anthology of weather.
The country has you somehow at its mercy.
The size of the moon begins to matter,
and every night, a whippoorwill leaves omens.

All names are hung on stilted mailboxes,
spasmodically fed with last week's letters.
The children quickly learn to wave.
A summer changes strangers into neighbors.

Here, one is grateful to the tolerant landscape,
and glad to be known by men with leather faces
who welcome anything but questions.
Words, like the water, must be used with care.

III

FOUR FIGURES FOR THE SEA

I

Inside the crook of the blackened beckoning headland
five winters since, the sea drew down this drifter.
        The drowned hull found the sand.

Five winters' water and the tides' long fingers
undressed like nibbling fish its driftwood ribwork.
        Barnacles cobbled the keel.

Overboard now, in weeded prisms of water
the crusted woodwork hulk wavers, forever
            safe in the fossiling sea.

Stilled like the little galleons old men's fingers
bottled and sealed, it lies, a sand-shelved skeleton
            stayed in the glass-topped bay.

So in the glass of words, I stay the sea.

II

We only remembered the sea in his faraway eyes.
But under a sailing moon, on cots of foam,
the sea brought back his sodden, foundered body.
    The long waves rolled him home.

All the long night, he drowned in our waterlogged nightmares.
The swollen tide drained out of his flooded heartbeat.
Nightlong, he lay beside the subsiding water
    and the sea ran out of his eyes.

III

Here is the shell, the sea made flesh, and spinning
through threaded webs and whorls
flowered in your giant fingers,
your history is this graph
of graven hieroglyphics.
These intricate pink nets
hold change and chart your life.
Tracing the lacy spiral,
enmeshed, the eye turns inward.
The heart of the shell is shadow.
Inside, you cannot see.
But listen, ear to the sea's ear,
and hear, rising and falling,
the pulse at the turning center —
your heartbeat and the sea.

IV

Over the walking foreshore cluttered
black with the tide's untidy wrack,
and pools that brimmed with the moon,
I tresspassed underwater.
My feet stained seabed sand.
The night wore guilt like a watermark;
and down the guilty dark,
the gulls muttered to windward.
Far out, the tide spoke back.

Across the morning clean of my walking
ghost and the driftwood litter,
singly I walked into singing light.
The rocks walked light on the water;
and clouds as clean as spinnakers
puffed in the sea-blue sky.
A starfish signed the sand. Beyond
I faced the innocent sea.

UNDERWORLD

Sailors will tumble an old boat head over heel
for a turtle-turned house, and crazily cut a door
in its planks. They take the underside deck for a floor
and poke two pottering chimney pipes through the keel
for their driftwood fires. They have hammock beds, and a hatch,
and sea-gear— but never they know, as they lie unsleeping,
their hull-home is haunted by waterless old wood, weeping
when the clock goes wild, ringing bells at the turn of the watch.

Because of the crime of changing a ship-shaped thing
so suddenly into a lurching hunchbacked shelter,
I'd be afraid, so afraid of the sea at evening,
afraid of the portholes, to find fish goggling there,
and a green strange undersea light beginning to filter
in through some drowned man's seaweed-swirling hair.

THE SEASONS OF THE SEA

The cycle of the water rolling landwards
is shaped in the sailor's tale of a mother sea
and the eyes of men remembering their islands
from the harbour-masted wharves of a huddled town
    on a windy coast where the beating tides
break into births and deaths on beginning beaches
with mourning gulls to tell the nine waves' labour

To a boy by the tarry wood of the knotted pierstakes
lost in the windward look of a sailor dream
when the hymns from the churchlit windows danced on the water
she would come with the thud of men going down to the dawn
    their rubber boots stubbing the grubby decks
of the boats that nibbled their ropes with a rusty ringbolt
waiting with whining wire at the water's end

And later as lad unloading the groaning hold
he would taste the salt that crisped on hands as her knife
slit into the slithering breasts and her limber fingers
danced in the nimble nets for a whistling price
    blowing a kiss to the luck of the catch
as she counted the tumbling fish that gasped to death
in the round and bountiful basins and boxes of salt

Under the lingering looks from the buzzing pierhead
when she walked there the bay would wrinkle with voices
from the rocking boats that she loved with her eyes
in the playing water by the knocking spar
    with blown hair sprayed on the wind as her word
silenced the swarthy men in their black desiring
when she laughed with her teeth the length of a limb away

    Until the nights in the netted loft when as maiden
she would sink in the swimming moon and make a prayer
of the tides of her heart to take her breathing lover
the boy with secrets to find in her skylight bed
    wound in a net of moonlit limbs
all the loose winds would lie with her kissing mouth
to drown his boyhood in her fumbled hair

    A seawife's curse on children born in a storm
by draughty lamps in the doom of a harbour home
with her motherhood wet on her hardened hands she suffered
her luckless urchin on a turning tide
    on the ebb of a love that spilt and spent
its warmth on the twisted mouths of barren women
changing the joy of the loins to a waterfront shame

    After to dread her name in the shipyard whisper
of lips by the lamps to lure the emptying men
with oaths on their mouths and dirty sailor money
for easy love below a drunken moon
    friendly legs in a brassbound bed
and her morning strut beneath the leering mastheads
buying the eyes of the lads with a crimson tune

At the last to grow in the lying lovers' moon
to the sight of a fishless sea and the sense of a grief
that sank in the net as she took the touch of ages
and lay alone in the pool of a cycle life
    and all the moons and crossing tides
talked in a graveyard sleep to tell her children
the tidy words above her driftwood stone

    And fishbones white in the silt of a seaweed harbour
    will take the tale to its end on a drying bay
    to begin again in the ooze of a tide returning
    to crabs in the pools and pockets of the rock
        linking the chain of the baffled love
that anchors the endless man to his sailor living
alone in a loft with the fish falling back in the sea

THE WATERGLASS

A church tower crowned the town,
double in air and water,
and over anchored houses
the round bells rolled at noon.
Bubbles rolled to the surface.
The drowning bells swirled down.

A sun burned in the bay.
A lighthouse towered downward,
moored in the mirroring fathoms.
The seaweed swayed its tree.
A boat below me floated
upside down on the sky.

An underwater wind
ruffled the red-roofed shallows,
where wading stilt-legged children
stood in the clouded sand,
and down from the knee-deep harbour
a ladder led to the drowned.

Gulls fell out of the day.
The thrown net met its image
in the window of the water.
A ripple slurred the sky.
My hand swam up to meet me,
and I met myself in the sea.

Mirrored, I saw my death
in the underworld in the water,
and saw my drowned face sway in
the glass day underneath—
till I spoke to my speaking likeness,
and the moment broke with my breath.

DIRECTIONS FOR A MAP

I

Birds' eyes see almost this, a tidy island
dropped like a footprint on a painted sea.
But maps set margins. Here, the land is measured,
changed to a flat, explicit world of names.

Crossing the threads of roads to tattered coastlines,
the rivers run in veins that crack the surface.
Mountains are dark like hair, and here and there
lakes gape like moth holes with the sea showing through.

Between the seaports tiptoe dotted shiplines
crossing designs of latitude and language.
The towns are wearing names. The sea is titled.
A compass stamps the corner like a seal.

Distance is spelt in alphabets and numbers.
Arrows occur at intervals of inches.
There are no signs for love or trouble, only
dots for a village and a cross for churches.

Here space is free for once from time and weather.
The sea has paused. To plot is possible.
Given detachment and a careful angle,
all destinations are predictable.

And given, too, the confidence of distance,
strangers may take a hundred mural journeys.
For once the paths are permanent, the colors
outlast the seasons and the death of friends.

44

And even though, on any printed landscape,
directions never tell you where to go,
maps are an evening comfort to the traveler:
a pencil line will quickly take him home.

II

Afraid at first,
they hid from that enormous, nameless sky.

Beyond their well-known neighbourly horizons,
anyone was a stranger, dangerous,
possibly armed, and never to be trusted.
Only the sailors brought back stories, roaring
news of the drunken east. What was the sea?
Water, they hoped. But not true blue.
Deceitful as a drug, a chronic liar.
Their gods were often angry. Notwithstanding,
a globe was growing strangely in their heads.
   A few had dreamed and listened.
Ptolemy, telling the sun on the blank sand,
was not afraid to say *incognitus*
   and keep his head.
Meanwhile, the earth was anybody's guess.
Mercator, straightening a later landscape,
crisscrossing Europe with meridians,
was hardly happy. Trouble and his errors
gathered like cobwebs in his attic rooms.
Only old Blaeu, below his golden sundial,
made peace with all the angels.
What was a map? His brush moved through blue water
and soothed the vellum sea. His eyes were azure.

Letters paced out his oceans. Thumbnail galleons
stayed everlastingly in sight of land.
The unknown poles were playgrounds laid for dolphins.
Alone, his wonder easily unwound
a starred and palette-colored world
on charts as haunted as a mermaid's dream.

   But still the unfathomed, many-monstered sea
took toll, and tightened sailors' mouths.
Now there were charts to blame. Over their names,
the waves wore numbers, therefore errors.
Fear faltered still too often on the tiller,
till the instruments took over—
astrolabes stabbing at the sky for figures,
safe from all human failing and from hearsay,
the trade routes flagged with information,
the poles stuck thick with banners, and
the compass turning permanently home.
The figured winds withdrew, and Atlas rested,
the globe no longer heavy on his hands.
Down went Atlantis, mourned by dreamers,
greener among the skulls and mouldered bones.
The crest of Everest alone resisted.
Where was there left to go? We held the world.
      Light years away, in space,
some star was winking like an eager girl.

Light years away, but here, we stared
across the abyss between the map and us,
and wondered what was missing. In the nights,
nightmares knocked often in our heads, our days

were just as difficult. The end, we found,
was not a map, but here, and a beginning.
So we had guessed.
                    But looking backwards,
we missed the comfort of the old illusions,
the tall alleviating gods, the travellers;
and, mindful of those faithful days,
we often wished for angels in the wind—
come back, old Boreas, even you are welcome;
Zephryus merry in the west, young Auster,
sunbearing Eurus, we remember you.

III

Look through the map at now. This present island
wakes and takes on an unpredictable day.
Thin mists are nuzzling the uncanny mountains.
A boat is trying its luck on the knitted bay.

Birds blow about. Northwards, a wind is rising.
By the wall, the woolen sheep are keeping warm.
The sun makes patchwork on the oatmeal meadow.
The clouds take up positions for a storm.

Here we have never been. These moors are strangers.
The road we guessed is lost beyond the hill.
Miles have no meaning now. The gulls are frightened.
There are no arrows other than the will.

Names will not help. The signpost chokes with ivy.
Lightning winks. The sky is coming down.
The map is pocked with rain, and clapping thunder
calls time to ships across the rain-crossed town.

Somewhere behind a blurring village window,
a traveller waits. The storm walks in his room.
Under his hand, a lamplit map is lying.
Pencils tonight will never take him home.

I V

Across the plot of the land
falls the long shadow of the pilgrim hand.
A wind in miniature, the breath
troubles that country as withdrawn as death.
Though, safe from weather and the ways of love,
these maps will never move,
the moving eyes, the island in the mind
have their own maps to find.

*So grant to us again
the courage to begin,
to wish the morning well,
to kiss before we tell,
to trust enough to choose,
to take our days as news.*

*Here, in this trackless time,
where habit is our crime,
the amazing day begins,
forgiving us our sins,
and as we turn to bless,
the landscape answers Yes.*

V

A globe-eyed child finds first a map for wonder.
Her sea is scribbled full of ship-shaped fish.
Playing with all the names like spells, she tells
the time in Spain, and sails her fingers south.
Europe is torn: the world has no dimensions.
America is half the size of Rome.
Also, since here is now, all maps are nowhere.
This is a wishing world, where towns are home.

She marks a cross for luck, and lastly colors
a puff-cheeked cherub in the bottom corner—

     which terrifies a folded fly
who, tired from crawling foodless over Europe,
was crouching in the margin, contemplating
the little cipher of the maker's name.

MAINE COAST

These islands are all anchored deep dark down.
Pines pitch-thick, gnarled green, and rich of root,
logs lying, lopped boughs, branches, broken rock,
the bow of a boat, the length of a life, weed-water.
I am an island, this is nearest home.

Time is called morning, clinging moist, mist-ridden.
Days are disguised, the houses are half trees —
wind in the attic, sea in the cellar, words
all alien. Though sun burns books, blinds eyes,
I see through to the bone and the beginning.

Tomorrow waits for the net; today tells
time in circles on the trunks, in tides.
Boats are lucky, love is lucky, children
are kings — and we must listen to the wise
wind saying all our other lives are lies.

ISLE OF ARRAN

Where no one was was where my world was stilled
into hills that hung behind the lasting water,
a quiet quilt of heather where bees slept,
and a single slow bird in circles winding
round the axis of my head.

Any wind being only my breath, the weather
stopped, and a woolen cloud smothered the sun.
Rust and a mist hung over the clock of the day.
A mountain dreamed in the light of the dark
and marsh mallows were yellow for ever.

Still as a fish in the secret loch alone
I was held in the water where my feet found ground
and the air where my head ended,
all thought a prisoner of the still sense—
till a butterfly drunkenly began the world.

TO LIGHTEN MY HOUSE

Somehow come to the calm of this present, a sunday in summer,
here, held and steady under the spread sky,
    I set this christened poem loose
        to lighten my house.

Rising, my eyes and the sea, for ever and this time more,
meet; and across the anonymous sea-shaped bay,
    the wind, my life, and the ground beneath
        all turn on this breath.

Far away, over several lives and this sea, Scotland is aging,
the shape of a humped sea-horse, mountain-headed,
    holding that kind and harboured home
        where I found my name,

on the inherited, mapped island I loved by its first name,
Arran, hunchbacked and hazy with family secrets,
    where, quartered in tidy seasons, I woke
        into shelters of talk.

My father's grave voice preaching, in a parish rich with fishermen,
the chanted parables for faith, while a dark god
    stormed in the unworded nights and wild eyes
        of the boy I was,

the hard-bitten heather on hills, the drowned bird nursed like a sister
wearing death in its sweet breast, all spelled my fear
    on the frightened nightfalling sea where I sailed,
        growing up and growing old —

years where my head, turned loose in burning chapels of doubt,
turned back on my blood, with all the words for journeys—
    war, and a war in my body to break
        that one way back.

I tell my stilled years to the sea, but the sea moves and is patient,
bearing all bottled wishes, faithful to all its fables,
    promising islands that will ask me back
        to take my luck.

Yet not in these seafared years, borne now in all my choices,
but in this firstborn day, in my opened house,
    are my hands handed the chance to love
        down one dear life.

And patiently into my bruised dark house, light breaks like a birthday
as, shouldering the weather of this place, I wake in
    the nowhere of the moment, single-willed
        to love the world.

COLOPHON

Eight hundred and fifty copies of this book
have been designed and hand set in Garamond
type by Barbara Morgan and Marian Bryan.
The printing has been done by The Morgan Press
and the binding by the J. F. Tapley Company.